Sugar Inspira

Wedding Flower Sprays

CLAIRE WEBB

'On Top of the World's Best Selling Cakes'

Dedication

This book is dedicated to Rachael, for her continued support and friendship, and to Julian, with thanks for the endless help and time they have both given me.

First published 1997 by Merehurst Limited.
This edition printed 2003 for Culpitt Limited.
Reprinted 2005, 2007.

Merehurst is an imprint of Murdoch Books® UK Ltd

A catalogue record of this book is available from the British Library.

Editor: Helen Southall
Design: Anita Ruddell
Photographer: James Duncan

Colour separation by Bright Arts, Hong Kong
Printed in China

Contents

Introduction

Beautifully arranged sprays of flowers are an important part of any wedding, and sugar flowers make perfect keepsakes afterwards.

When I was asked to write this book I decided to have a closer look at the flowers today's brides are carrying in their bouquets. Roses, carnations, lilies, freesias and foliage are still popular, but some people these days are being slightly more adventurous and choosing less traditional flowers, such as sunflowers and clematis. With this in mind, I have tried to cover various techniques for making sprays using both traditional and 'modern' flowers, with a range of ideas for assembling them.

Wedding sprays can contain any type of flowers once the basic shape has been mastered, and as long as there are focal points to work from. Sugar flowers are a popular choice on wedding cakes, and they can also be used as table decorations and to make pretty wedding favours.

I hope as you progress through this book you will gain confidence in arranging your sprays of flowers and will perhaps try some of the ideas using alternative flowers.

Equipment

Much of the equipment used to make the flowers and sprays in this book is basic sugar flower-making equipment, all of which is available from good sugarcraft suppliers (see page 48). Templates are provided for some of the less readily available cutters.

Board and rolling pin

There is now a wide range of boards and pins on the market. I still prefer to use a plain non-stick board and pin, although grooved versions of both are available. These leave ridges in the rolled-out paste ready for inserting wires. Also available are 'mexican hat' boards that have different-sized holes in them for making the various flowers.

Pads

Again, a range of pads is now available, some with holes and some without. They are very useful when shaping and softening cut-out petals or leaves.

Paintbrushes

I use mainly flat 5mm (¼ inch) brushes for dusting, usually made from sable or a sable/synthetic blend. Much more control can be exercised, and a better finish achieved, using brushes of this sort.

A selection of very fine paintbrushes is also required for adding detail. Again, it is best to choose sable brushes for this.

Modelling tools

The main tools used in this book are:
Dogbone tool Used to cup and soften the edges of petals and leaves;
Dresden tool Mainly used to hollow and vein;
Craft knife For cutting around templates, etc.

Veiners

There is a huge selection of veiners on the market now and most of them are readily available. However they can quite easily be made by sticking real leaves and petals on to a backing of lightweight card.

Cutters

I use cutters to achieve basic shapes, and then these can be further formed and shaped by hand. Cutters are available in both metal and plastic; it is a matter of personal preference which you use (I work with both types).

Wires

Green and white wires are available in a wide range of thicknesses. 'Scientific' wire is a covered wire that is very fine and flexible. Fine florists' wire is also useful.

Other equipment required

You will also need: florists' tape (green and white), tweezers, fine scissors, cocktail sticks (toothpicks) with one point filed to a smooth, blunt end, stamens, wire cutters, cotton thread, egg white or gum glue (page 46), confectioners' glaze (page 6) and flower paste (page 46).

For assembling posies/sprays, the following are required: florists' tape (preferably the papery sort), tweezers and wire cutters. A tape shredder is useful for cutting florists' tape to a narrower width (I always work with ½ or ⅓-width tape), but a pair of sharp scissors also does the job. Posy picks are used to hold flower sprays firmly in cakes. They also protect cakes from wire corrosion. Additional 18-gauge wires are occasionally used for strengthening stems.

Techniques
Colouring

Paste and powder colourings give the best results. Both can be

used to colour the flower paste before rolling, although I favour paste colouring for this. Always colour the paste a lighter shade than required for the finished flower. This leaves the flower or leaf stronger as the paste has less colour to absorb, and it allows for more scope when colouring with dusting powders (petal dusts/blossom tints).

Both paste and powder colours can be used for painting fine details on to assembled flowers, simply by adding a small amount of water or clear alcohol (gin or vodka) to the

colour. Liquid colours can also be used in this way.

The following colours have been used to complete the flowers in this book:

Acorn: paste colour – cream; non-toxic gold paint
Alstroemeria (flowers, leaves and buds): paste colours – daffodil, Christmas green, brown; dusting powders – daffodil, holly/ivy, thrift, spring green; liquid colour – claret/cyclamen
Carnation: paste colour – daffodil; dusting powder – marigold
Casablanca lily: paste colours – paprika, white, Christmas

5

green; dusting powders – brown, spring green, snow

Clematis (flowers and leaves): paste colours – pink, Christmas green; dusting powders – pink and white mixed, holly/ivy

Eucalyptus: paste colours – bluebell, Christmas green, pink mixed; dusting powders – dark eucalyptus, black, cyclamen, autumn green mixed

Freesia (flowers and buds): paste colours – cream, white, Christmas green; dusting powders – forsythia, autumn green

Jasmine: paste colour – white; dusting powder – holly/ivy

Longiflorum lily: paste colours – white, yellow, pale green; dusting powders – spring green, lemon, snow

Orchids and filler flowers: paste colour – cream; liquid colour – claret/cyclamen; dusting powders – chestnut and cyclamen mixed

Rose (cream): paste colours – cream, Christmas green; dusting powders – champagne, holly/ivy, thrift

Rose (open): paste colours – daffodil, Christmas green; dusting powders – coral, holly/ivy

Rose (red): paste colours – red compound, Christmas green; dusting powders – red, cyclamen, thrift, holly/ivy

Sunflower: paste colours – daffodil, Christmas green, dark brown; dusting powders – sunflower, daffodil, holly/ivy

Glazing

Finished petals and leaves can be glazed in several ways, but I find the following methods best:

Steaming

After dusting leaves and petals, pass them briefly through the steam from a boiling kettle. This will give a slight sheen and help prevent tiny fragments of dusting powder (petal dust/blossom tint) from falling on to the surface of the cake.

Confectioners' glaze

Confectioners' varnish is available from sugarcraft suppliers and can be used at full or half strength, the latter giving a less harsh shine. To make half-strength glaze, place 3 teaspoons of varnish in a small jar. Gradually add 2 teaspoons of clear alcohol (gin or vodka), shaking well between each addition to prevent the varnish from 'sponging'.

Making leaves

Leaves are a very important part of any floral design. Without realistic foliage and the correct balance, an arrangement can lose its overall impact. The basic technique for making leaves is the same; only the shape, colour and veins tell them apart. Cutters are now available for most leaves, but for those that are not available, templates will have to be made. All green leaves are made from paste coloured with Christmas green, then dusted using a selection of green dusting powders (petal dusts/blossom tints), such as holly/ivy, moss, ruskus and autumn green. Choose the colour that is the closest match to the plant. Brown leaves are made from cream paste, then dusted with a selection of brown and rust dusting powders, such as bulrush, chestnut and cream.

Basic method

1 Roll out thinly a piece of flower paste in the required colour, leaving a narrow ridge of thicker paste down the centre. Cut out the leaf shape required.

2 Dip a wire of the appropriate gauge into egg

white or gum glue. (I generally use 28-gauge wires, but larger leaves may require 24 or 26-gauge wires.) Hold the leaf between your index finger and thumb, and insert the wire into the paste ridge. Vein with leaf veiners.

3 Soften the edge of the leaf with a dogbone tool. Give the leaf a little movement by twisting it, and leave to dry overnight. Dust and glaze as required.

Linear (lily) leaves

1 Roll a piece of green flower paste into a sausage. Dip a 28-gauge wire into egg white or gum glue, and pull it lengthways through the centre of the paste.

2 Place the paste on a non-stick board and flatten it slightly. Roll the paste as thinly as possible either side of the wire (from the centre to the outside edges) using a piece of dowel or a mini rolling pin.

3 Cut out the shape required (for lily leaves, see template on page 47) using a pair of scissors or a craft knife, then vein using a dresden tool. Soften the edges with a dogbone tool. Leave to dry, then dust and glaze as required.

Making ribbon bows

Swallow-tail

Fold a piece of ribbon in half. Cut a piece of 30-gauge wire and

wind one end around the bottom of the ribbon approximately three times. Trim the ends of the ribbon to a point. The swallow-tail is usually used at the tip of a flower spray.

Double bounce bow

Form a length of ribbon into two loops next to one another – the loops should appear heart-shaped. Make a third loop next to the first two, but make it double the size. Wrap a piece of 30-gauge wire around the ribbon approximately three times. Cut the largest loop in half with scissors and trim the ends to a point. For shorter tails, make all three loops the same size. Bounce bows are used mainly for filling gaps in sprays. Long-

tailed bows are quite often used around the base of a posy.

Figure-of-eight bows

Hold a length of ribbon in one hand and, with your other hand, form a loop at the opposite end. Hold the middle of the ribbon between your thumb and index finger. Keep the ribbon flat to itself, and make a loop at the other end. With the same piece of ribbon, make another two loops in the same way. Fold the ribbon in half and secure a piece of 30-gauge wire at the bottom; trim the ends of the ribbon to a point. Figure-of-eight bows are usually used when a larger gap needs to be filled. Several bows can be placed together at the top end of a spray.

Casablanca Lily

Symbolizing purity and modesty, lilies can be used to dramatic effect.

Materials

Flower paste
Paste and powder colours,
page 6
26-gauge green wires
Egg white or gum glue
30-gauge green and white wires
Small amount of royal icing

Equipment

Florists' tape (green)
Tiger lily cutters (424–425)
Dogbone tool
Veiner or dresden tool
No. 0 piping tube (tip)

1 To make the pistil, roll a small piece of pale green flower paste into a sausage. Dip a 26-gauge wire into egg white or gum glue, and pull it lengthways through the centre of the paste. Taper the paste at both ends, keeping it smooth all the way up. Make the top of the pistil by shaping a small piece of paste into a trefoil and attaching it to the top of the wired paste using egg white or gum glue. The pistil should be about two-thirds the length of the petals.

2 To make the stamens, cut six pieces of 30-gauge green wire 7.5cm (3 inches) long. Bend 5mm (¼ inch) wire over at a right angle at one end of each wire. Bend this short piece back on itself to form a 'T' shape.

3 Roll six tiny pieces of rust-coloured flower paste into sausage shapes, tapering both ends of each to a point. Attach these to the 'T'-shaped wires. When dry, brush some egg white or gum glue over the paste and dip into brown dusting powder (petal dust/blossom tint). Tape the stamens around the pistil at equal intervals.

4 Roll out some white flower paste, leaving a ridge of thicker paste in the centre. Cut out three wide and three narrow petals with the tiger lily cutters and insert a moistened 30-gauge white wire. Using a dogbone tool, frill the edges of each petal. Vein the petals with a veiner or dresden tool. Curl the tips outwards, and leave to dry.

5 Mark in the central vein of each petal with bright green dusting powder. Dust the petals with white lustre, and pipe on tiny dashes of white royal icing near the base and up towards the tip of each petal. Tape the three widest petals underneath the stamens and position the remaining three in the gaps below these.

Casablanca Lily Spray

Flowers

8 lily leaves, page 7
5 casablanca lilies, page 8
9 sprays dried gypsophila, see Note

1 Tape two leaves together, one above the other. Place one lily in the centre of the leaves and arrange three pieces of gypsophila behind.

2 Position a further two lilies in the spray, one to the left and the other to the right. Attach another two leaves to the right and a piece of gypsophila in between the two lilies. Position the next lily at the back of the spray and over to the left, along with two more leaves.

3 Place a piece of gypsophila behind the two back lilies. Tape the last lily at the back of the spray towards the right and slightly lower than the others. Secure four pieces of gypsophila at the back of the spray and add another two leaves to finish.

Note

Dried gypsophila is used to fill out many of the sprays in this book. It can be bought in bunches, each stem bearing small florets. Simply cut off each floret and attach to a 30-gauge wire with florists' tape. Steam the gypsophila lightly to swell the flowers.

Casablanca Lily Cake

Considered lucky by many, a horseshoe-shaped cake makes an interesting variation.

Materials

20cm (8 inch) horseshoe-shaped cake
Apricot glaze
1kg (2lb) marzipan (almond paste)
1.25kg (2½lb) white sugarpaste (rolled fondant)
White royal icing
Clear alcohol (gin or vodka)

Equipment

28cm (11 inch), 30cm (12 inch) oval cake boards
Icing smoothers
Paper piping bags
Nos. 1 and 43 piping tubes (tips)
173cm (68 inches) 3mm wide ribbon to trim cake
183cm (72 inches) 15mm wide ribbon to trim board
Double-sided tape
Posy pick

Flowers

Casablanca Lily Spray, page 9

Note

Do not coat this cake too thickly with marzipan and icing, or it will not fit on the top board. Alternatively, use a size larger for both boards.

Preparation

1 Brush the cake with apricot glaze, cover with marzipan, and allow to dry. Coat both the cake boards with sugarpaste and set aside. When they are both dry, stick them together with a little royal icing, lining them up at one end and forming a 'step' at the other. Set aside.

2 Brush the marzipan with clear alcohol and coat the cake with sugarpaste. When firm, transfer the cake to the cake board.

Decoration

3 Using white royal icing and a no. 43 piping tube, pipe a snail's trail around the base of the cake. Attach two lines of narrow ribbon above this and secure with royal icing. Using a no. 1 piping tube, pipe a random dot pattern on the surface of the cake.

4 Attach the wide ribbon to the cake boards using double-sided tape. Insert a posy pick in the top of the cake and insert the spray of flowers into this, using royal icing to secure if necessary. Arrange the spray so that the flowers fall into the horseshoe.

Alstroemeria

Alstroemerias are also known as Peruvian lilies.

Materials

Scientific wire
Egg white or gum glue
Flower paste
Paste and powder colours,
page 5
26, 30 and 33-gauge white wires
Claret/cyclamen liquid colour
Clear alcohol (gin or vodka)

Equipment

Florists' tape (white and green)
Fine scissors
Cocktail stick (toothpick)
Alstroemeria cutters (436–437)
Alstroemeria veiners
Angled tweezers

Stamens and pistil

1 Cut five pieces of scientific wire, each 4cm (1½ inches) long. Hook one end of each, dip in egg white or gum glue and attach a small drop-shaped piece of brown flower paste to each. Leave to dry.

2 To make the pistil, cut a 10cm (4 inch) length of 30-gauge white wire. Attach a piece of ⅓-width white florists' tape, leaving approximately 5mm (¼ inch) excess at the top. Cut this into three with fine scissors, and twist each to form little spines. Curl the ends around a cocktail stick.

3 Tape the stamens to the pistil approximately 2.5cm (1 inch) down its wire. Bend the stamens and pistil down slightly at the join.

Petals

4 Roll out some pale yellow flower paste very finely, leaving a ridge of thicker paste down the centre. Cut three wide and three narrow petals. Insert a moistened 5cm (2 inch) length of 33-gauge wire approximately 5mm (¼ inch) into each petal. Vein, and gently frill the edges with a cocktail stick.

5 With scissors, trim the base of each petal near the wire to a point. This will prevent excess bulk at the base of the flower. Leave to dry with the petals curving outwards.

6 Dust the petals and paint on the dots, using claret/cyclamen liquid colour mixed with a little alcohol.

Assembly

7 Tape the narrow petals to the stamens, two above and one below. Tape the wider petals behind, in the gaps.

8 Shape a pea-sized piece of green flower paste into an oval and slide it up behind the petals. With tweezers, pinch grooves lengthways into this.

Buds

9 Mould a piece of pale green flower paste into a long oval, and pinch it into a slightly triangular shape. Insert a moistened 26-gauge wire.

10 With a craft knife, cut three deep cuts lengthways down the bud. Using tweezers, pinch six ridges at the base. Leave to dry. Dust the buds with dark green and burgundy.

Alstroemeria Spray

Flowers

5 alstroemeria flowers, page 12
4 alstroemeria buds, left
6 cream roses, page 32
14 stems eucalyptus (varying lengths), page 14
20 sprays dried gypsophila, page 9

1 Start with one stem of eucalyptus, about 10cm (4 inches) long, and tape to it two alstroemeria buds, a small one at the bottom and a larger one just

higher and slightly to the right. Attach another stem of eucalyptus, about 5cm (2 inches) long, to the right.

2 Secure a rose in the centre, then attach another alstroemeria bud to the right and another behind the rose to the left. Add a stem of eucalyptus, about 5cm (2 inches) in length, on the left, beside the rose.

3 Position two pieces of gypsophila underneath the rose, and place another rose to

13

the right with a piece of gypsophila and a small piece of eucalyptus to the left.

4 Select an alstroemeria flower, preferably one that is not too open, and position this above the eucalyptus on the left. Attach a piece of gypsophila to its right with a small piece of eucalyptus underneath. Add another piece of gypsophila to the right. Attach a piece of gypsophila to the right of the alstroemeria and place another alstroemeria to the left; tape another small piece of eucalyptus to the left of the alstroemeria. Secure four separate pieces of gypsophila over the top of the alstroemerias. This completes the bottom part of the spray.

Tape the wires so they are tidy and bend them at a right angle.

5 Take three pieces of gypsophila and tape them together. Arrange the three remaining alstroemerias around this to make a circle. Add three short pieces of eucalyptus in the gaps and secure a piece of gypsophila underneath them.

6 Join the two parts of the spray together. Add a stem of eucalyptus and gypsophila on each side of the two sprays to fill the gap.

7 Finally, position three stems of eucalyptus towards the back of the spray and attach four roses in the gaps.

Eucalyptus

The subtle grey-green of eucalyptus makes it useful filler foliage. Roll out grey-green flower paste, leaving a ridge down the centre. Cut out leaf shapes using round metal cutters (292-295) or templates

(page 47). If using round cutters, bend them into a slightly more oval shape to match the templates. Insert moistened 30-gauge wires. Soften the edges and vein. Shape the leaves and pinch a tiny point at the top. When dry, dust (page 6). To assemble, tape two small leaves to the top of a 30-gauge wire. Continue down the stem, graduating leaves as you progress. Dust the stems with burgundy.

Opposite: Alstroemeria Bell Cake (page 16)

Alstroemeria Bell Cake

A bell is an unusual shape for a cake,
suitable for a small wedding or an anniversary.

Materials

20cm (8 inch) bell-shaped cake
Apricot glaze
2.5kg (5lb) marzipan (almond paste)
3kg (6lb) cream sugarpaste (rolled fondant)
Clear alcohol (gin or vodka)
Cream royal icing

Equipment

25cm (10 inch) round cake board
Icing smoothers
Paper piping bags
Nos. 42 and 1.5 piping tubes (tips)
Tracing paper
Pencil
Scriber
92cm (3 feet) 15mm wide ribbon to trim board
Double-sided tape
Posy pick

Flowers

Alstroemeria Spray, page 13

Preparation

1 Brush the cake with apricot glaze and cover with marzipan. Allow to dry. Coat the cake board with sugarpaste and set aside.

2 Brush the marzipan with clear alcohol and coat the cake with sugarpaste. When firm, transfer the cake to the board.

Decoration

3 Using cream royal icing and a no. 42 piping tube, pipe a snail's trail around the base of the cake.

4 Trace the patterns on page 47 and scribe on to the bottom of the cake and the cake board. Pipe in the patterns using a no. 1.5 piping tube.

5 Attach the ribbon to the cake board using double-sided tape.

6 Insert a posy pick in the top of the cake, and insert the flower spray into this, using a little royal icing to secure it if necessary.

Sunflower

Bright and cheerful, sunflowers are becoming a popular choice for weddings.

Materials

18-gauge green wires
Flower paste
Paste and powder colours,
page 6
Egg white or gum glue
Cel block
Cardamom seeds
Brown textured powder

Equipment

Florists' tape (green)
Kitchen foil
Paper clip
Orchid petal cutter from set
19–21
Orchid petal veiner
Thin foam
Craft knife
Sunflower leaf cutters
(702–703)
Ivy leaf cutters (580–582)
Ivy leaf veiners
Dogbone tool
Needle or pin

Stem

1 Tape together three pieces of 18-gauge wire, each approximately 20cm (8 inches) in length, leaving 2.5cm (1 inch) untaped at the top. Bend the three untaped sections outwards.

2 Roll out some green flower paste and cut out two circles. (The exact size is not important – about 5cm/2 inch diameter.) Thread one of the green circles up the stem, underneath the wires, and secure the other on top, using egg white or gum glue. Cut a large circle of foil, fold it into a cone shape, and slip it up the stem underneath the green circles. Keep it in place with a paper clip. (This helps to hold the shape of the sunflower petals.) Leave to dry.

Petals

3 Using the orchid petal cutter and bright yellow flower paste, cut and vein the petals – two or three can be made at a time. Soften the edges with a dogbone tool. Stick petals all the way round just inside the rim of the top circle, making sure they do not touch. Leave to dry.

4 Add another layer of petals, this time placing them just inside the first layer and in between the original petals. Place very thin pieces of foam between the layers of petals, and leave in place until the paste is firm and dry.

5 Remove the foil. Dust the petals with sunflower, making the colour stronger at the base of each petal and lighter towards the tip.

Flower centre

6 Using a craft knife, cut a circle of Cel block, making it a little smaller than the green circles. Press the top edge

17

inwards with your thumbs to form a curved edge, so that the overall shape is that of a slight dome.

 Roll out a piece of brown flower paste and use it to cover the dome, securing with egg white or gum glue.

 Mix another small piece of brown paste with some egg white or gum glue to make a tacky glue. Spread this around the edge of the dome and stick cardamom seeds to it. When dry, brush egg white on the centre of the dome and sprinkle with brown textured powder. Leave to dry.

 When dry, use some more gum glue to attach the centre to the flower.

Leaves

 Both ivy leaves and sun-flower leaves are included in the Sunflower Spray (page 21). Make the leaves following the instructions on page 6, using sunflower and ivy leaf cutters and veiners. After dusting and steaming the ivy leaves, leave to dry, then use a needle or pin to scratch out the veins, revealing the paler base colour.

Freesia

In a spray, freesias can be used as stems or single flowers. Single flowers make useful and attractive fillers for larger sprays.

Materials

Small white stamens with heads removed
26 and 28-gauge wires
Egg white or gum glue
Paste and powder colours, page 6

Equipment

Florists' tape (green)
Fine scissors
Medium freesia cutter (F62, A.P.) or template, page 47
Dogbone tool
Cocktail stick (toothpick)
Dresden tool

Stamens

1 Attach four stamens to one end of a 26-gauge wire with ⅓ or ½-width tape. Leave one stamen higher than the others, and use a little extra tape to form a bulb at the base of the stamens. Flatten the top of the higher stamen and cut it into three with fine scissors.

2 Separate the stamens and brush the tips with egg white or gum glue, then dip these into powder colour to match the finished flower.

Petals

3 Roll out a piece of white flower paste quite thickly and, using a medium freesia cutter, cut out two shapes. Cover one, and soften the edges of the other using a dogbone tool. Place this on a firm board and separate the petals. Using the blunt end of a cocktail stick, apply pressure to the edges of the petals and roll outwards, leaving the paste in the centre a little thicker. When all three petals have been thinned, cup the ends with a dogbone tool.

19

Press the broad end of a dresden tool flat down the centre of each petal, then draw the top edges inwards slightly.

4 Brush egg white about a quarter of the way up each petal and at the base. Place the wired stamens on the petal shape with the bulb of tape just below the petals. Roll the petals to surround the centre. Hang the flower upside-down to dry.

5 Work the second shape in the same way as the first. Brush with egg white or gum glue and roll these around the first set of petals, making sure the petals lie in between the gaps in the first layer. Make secure. Hang the flower upside-down to dry, then dust with yellow.

Buds

6 As they grow, freesia buds change colour from green to the shade of the flower. To make a very small bud, form a piece of green flower paste into a cone. Place this on a 28-gauge hooked wire and roll it down between your thumb and index finger to form a slightly longer, slender bud.

7 Using cream flower paste mixed with a little green, make slightly larger buds in the same way, but make three cuts with a craft knife down the length of each bud.

8 To make buds that are about to open, form a piece of cream flower paste into a small round-ended shape and place on a hooked 26-gauge wire. Leave to dry. Using the medium freesia cutter, cut out one flower shape from white flower paste, and work as for the flower (see step 3, page 19). Wrap this around the bud shape and secure using egg white or gum glue. Allow to dry, then dust to match the flowers.

Calyx

9 Take a piece of green flower paste (slightly darker than that used for the small green buds) and make a cone shape. Open up the wide end using the point of a cocktail stick, then use a blunt cocktail stick to roll around the inside until you form a thin, hollow cone. Cut away two 'V' shapes from the sides of the cone, and thin the edges with the cocktail stick. Paint a little egg white or gum glue inside the calyx, push it up the wire and secure at the base of the flower or bud. (The smallest buds will nearly be covered by the calyx.)

Assembly

10 To make a stem of freesia, start by taping two small green buds next to one another; tape in further buds in increasing size until you reach the flowers. Tape in two or three flowers. The buds and flowers need to be taped one slightly to one side of the stem, and the next slightly to the other side, and so on down the stem. When the stem is complete, gently move the flowers and buds to form a natural-looking spray. Dust the calyxes bright green.

Sunflower Spray

Flowers

6 stems ivy leaves (varying
lengths), page 18
2 stems freesia, page 19
3 sunflowers, page 17
3 sunflower leaves (2 large,
1 small), page 18
4 stems dried gypsophila,
page 9

1 Take one stem of ivy and
one stem of freesia, both
approximately 12cm (5 inches)
in length. Secure the freesias on
top of the ivy approximately
2.5cm (1 inch) further down.
Bend both stems to the left in a
gentle curve.

2 Tape in a length of 18-
gauge wire to help
strengthen the stems. Take
another piece of ivy, approximately 7.5cm (3 inches) in
length, and attach this to the
right of the spray, and another
much smaller piece approximately 5cm (2 inches) in length,
to the left.

3 Attach the first sunflower
to the left and bend the
wire down at an angle of 45°.
Secure the second flower underneath this to the right of the
spray and the final flower below
the other two on the left.

4 Repeat steps 1 and 2, but
this time curve the spray
to the right. Add an 18-gauge
wire to strengthen as before.

5 Join the two sprays
together so they form an
'S' shape. Attach three sunflower leaves to the spray; the
small one should be placed
underneath the bottom flower
and the remaining two attached
at the join of the stems, under
the flowers.

6 Fill in the gaps between
the sunflowers with gyp-
sophila.

Sunflower Wedding Cake

The golden yellows of sunflowers and freesias, against a background of dark foliage, make this cake truly eye-catching.

Materials

20cm (8 inch), 25cm (10 inch)
teardrop-shaped cakes
Apricot glaze
1.75kg (3½ lb) marzipan
(almond paste)
2.25kg (4½ lb) cream sugarpaste
(rolled fondant)
Clear alcohol (gin or vodka)
Cream royal icing
Barber Folk paints

Equipment

20x25cm (8x10 inch), 20x30cm
(10x12 inch) oval cake boards
Icing smoothers
Paper piping bag
No. 42 piping tube (tip)
142cm (56 inches) 3mm wide
ribbon to trim cakes
Tracing paper
Pencil
Scriber
183cm (72 inches) 15mm wide
ribbon to trim boards
Double-sided tape
18cm (7 inch) clear perspex
pillar
1 large and 1 small Cel tube
cake stands

Flowers

Sunflower Spray, page 21

Preparation

1 Brush the cakes with apricot glaze, cover with marzipan, and allow to dry. Coat the cake boards with sugarpaste and set aside.

2 Brush the marzipan with alcohol and coat the cakes with sugarpaste. When firm, transfer the cakes to the cake boards.

Decoration

3 Using cream royal icing and a no. 42 piping tube, pipe a snail's trail around the base of each cake. Attach two lines of narrow ribbon above this and secure with royal icing.

4 Trace the sunflower design on page 47. Lay the tracing on the top of the small cake and very lightly scribe the pattern on to the surface. Using Barber Folk paints, paint in the sunflowers.

Finishing

5 Attach the ribbons to the cake boards using double-sided tape. Using a little gum glue, stick the pillar at the back of the large cake and leave to dry. Place the cakes on their stands. Very carefully place the flowers in the pillar, securing them with a little royal icing, if needed.

Clematis

This is based on the most common clematis, Montana rubens.

Materials

Cream cotton thread
Fine florists' wire
28-gauge green wires
Egg white or gum glue
Yellow textured powder
Flower paste
Paste and powder colours,
page 6

Equipment

Florists' tape (green)
Medium freesia cutter (F62,
A.P.) or template, page 47
Craft knife
Cocktail stick (toothpick)
Foam pad
Dresden tool
Leaf cutters (clematis montana
691–693) or templates, page 47

Stamens

1 Wind cream cotton thread around two fingers approximately 50 times. Remove and thread a piece of very fine florists' wire through the loop of cotton. Twist to secure. Repeat with another piece of wire at the other end of the loop, then fold the loop in half and cut through, making two sets of stamens.

2 Attach the stamens to 28-gauge wires using ⅓-width florists' tape. Immerse the cotton in egg white, then remove and leave to dry.

3 Use a pair of tweezers to pull the outside threads away from the centre. Trim the middle thread slightly shorter than the rest. Paint egg white or gum glue on to the ends of the cotton and dip them into yellow textured powder.

Petals

4 Roll out some pale pink flower paste, leaving the paste reasonably thick. Using the freesia cutter or template, cut out two shapes. Cut one petal from one of the shapes; discard the two that remain. Cut one petal from the other shape

and keep all three. You should now have four petals – two singles and one double.

5 Take each petal in turn and use the blunt end of a cocktail stick to thin down the edges. Start from the centre and use a rocking motion out towards one side. Return to the centre and repeat for the other side. Make sure the petals do not become too bulbous.

6 Place the petals on a foam pad and, using a dresden tool, vein the centre of each lengthways. Turn the petal over and, with the wider end of the

24

dresden tool, curl the petals inwards by stroking the paste from the edges.

7 Brush the wire below the stamens with a little egg white or gum glue. Wrap the double petals around the wire so they are opposite one another.

8 Position a single petal in each gap, securing with a little egg white or gum glue. Leave the flower upside-down for a short time, then turn it upright again. The petals should spray out to make an open flower. Leave to dry completely.

9 Dust the centre of the flower with a little green, and the petals with very pale pink.

Buds

10 Cut a piece of 28-gauge wire to approximately 10cm (4 inches) in length. Hook one end.

11 Make a small, slim cone from cream flower paste. Dip the wire into some egg white or gum glue, and insert it into the bottom of the cone. Mark four closed petals down the length of the cone with a craft knife. Leave to dry, then dust the buds with green and burgundy.

Leaves

12 Make clematis leaves following the instructions on page 6, and using the templates on page 47.

Clematis Spray

Flowers

9 stems clematis leaves
5 clematis buds,
5 clematis flowers

1 Tape two leaf stems together, one above the other, with the second one lower than the first and towards the right. Also tape in two buds, one higher than the other, and with the lowest to the right.

2 Attach another leaf stem to the left and a little lower than the previous leaves. Make sure the wire is forming a gentle curve to the right.

3 Leave a small gap and attach the first flower. Add a leaf stem and a bud to the left, and another spray of leaves a little lower on the right.

4 Position another flower in the centre of the spray, bending the wire down. Repeat steps 1–4, but leave out the leaves and bud in step 3.

5 Join the two sprays together, bending the wires as necessary, until the spray forms an attractive shape.

6 Finish the spray with the final flower positioned to the right of the centre. Attach a final set of leaves on the right.

Clematis Wedding Cake

This pretty two-tier cake is finished with frills
and two simple sprays of clematis.

Materials

15cm (6 inch), 23cm (9 inch)
heart-shaped cakes
Apricot glaze
1.6kg (3¼lb) marzipan (almond
paste)
2.25kg (4½lb) pale pink sugarpaste (rolled fondant)
Clear alcohol (gin or vodka)
Pale pink royal icing

Equipment

20cm (8 inch), 30cm (12 inch)
heart-shaped cake boards
Icing smoothers
Paper piping bag
No. 42 piping tube (tip)
244cm (96 inches) 3mm wide
ribbon to trim cakes
Scriber
Endless Garrett frill cutter with
scalloped blade
Cocktail stick (toothpick)
107cm (42 inches) 15mm wide
ribbon to trim boards
Double-sided tape
Posy pick
Perspex tilting cake stand

Flowers

2 Clematis Sprays, page 25

Preparation

1 Brush the cakes with apricot glaze, cover with marzipan, and allow to dry. Coat the cake boards with sugar-paste, and set aside.

2 Brush the marzipan with clear alcohol and coat the cakes with sugarpaste. When firm, transfer the cakes to the cake boards.

Decoration

3 Using pale pink royal icing and a no. 42 piping tube, pipe a snail's trail around the base of each cake. Attach two lines of narrow ribbon above this, securing with royal icing.

4 Scribe a line from the base of the point of each heart towards the top back edge on both sides of each cake. Cut out frills from sugarpaste using an endless Garrett frill cutter with a scalloped blade on the top edge. Frill the bottom edge with the blunt end of a cocktail stick. Attach to the cake with a little clear alcohol.

5 Attach the ribbons to the cake boards using double-sided tape.

6 Push a posy pick into the right-hand side of the small cake. Attach the small cake to a tilting stand (see Note). Position the stand in the centre of the large cake. Carefully insert one clematis spray in the posy pick, securing with royal icing if necessary. Secure the second spray on the board on the left of the large cake.

Note

To make sure the cake is secure on the tilting stand, follow the instructions carefully for drilling the cake board and using the pins that accompany the stand. Alternatively, glue a small piece of plastic right-angled strip (from DIY shops) to the back of the cake board, and hook it over the back of the stand to prevent the cake sliding off.

Carnation

Traditionally used for button-holes and bridal bouquets, carnations are here used to decorate the cake knife.

Materials

26-gauge green wires
Flower paste
Paste and powder colours,
page 5
Egg white or gum glue

Equipment

Florists' tape (green)
Blossom cutter (522)
Craft knife
Cocktail stick (toothpick)
Fine scissors
Abutilon leaf cutters or templates, page 47

Flower

1 Make a hook in a 26-gauge wire and wrap a length of ⅓-width tape round and round the hook until the wire resembles a match.

2 Roll out a piece of cream flower paste and cut out three shapes using a blossom cutter. Cover two of these and set aside. With a craft knife, make cuts towards the centre of the third shape to extend the indentations between the petals, then make a series of small cuts around the rounded edges of each petal. Frill the outside edge of the shape using a cocktail stick. Push the prepared wire through the centre of the shape. Paint some egg white or gum glue on one half of the shape only. When the shape is near the top of the wire, fold it upwards in half, then fold a quarter of the half to the centre and secure with egg white or gum glue. Turn the shape round and do the same with the remaining quarter.

3 Cut and frill a second shape. Push this up the wire behind the first layer and secure. Repeat with the final shape. Leave to dry.

Calyx

4 Form a piece of green flower paste into a cone. Hollow out the pointed end of the cone with a cocktail stick, making sure the edges are fine. With a fine pair of scissors, cut out five triangles from the top of the paste, then thin the points of the calyx with a cocktail stick. With egg white or gum glue, attach the calyx behind the flower. Make two nicks at the base of the calyx, on opposite sides, with the point of the scissors.

5 Dust the flower with dusting powder, making the edges of the petals darker.

Leaves

6 To accompany the carnations in the spray (page 30), make abutilon leaves following the instructions on page 6, and using abutilon leaf cutters or templates.

28

Jasmine

Often selected for bridal work, jasmine is delicate in both appearance and smell.

Materials

Flower paste
30-gauge green wires
Egg white or gum glue
Small white stamens

Equipment

Small Celstick
Stephanotis cutter (568)
Dogbone tool
Craft knife
Tweezers

Flower

1 Roll a small piece of white flower paste between your thumb and index finger to form a narrow tube. Flatten one end to form a base and roll out very finely with a small Celstick. Place a stephanotis cutter over the tube of paste and cut out the shape.

2 Soften the edges of the petals with a dogbone tool. Dip a piece of 30-gauge green wire into some egg white or gum glue and pull it through the centre of the flower.

3 Cut a stamen to approximately 5mm (¼ inch) in length. Insert this into the centre of the flower with a pair of tweezers, pressing to secure.

Calyx

4 Either paint five lines up the tube of the flower or make the calyx from a piece of dark green florists' tape approximately 5mm (¼ inch) in length. Cut one long edge of the tape into five sharp points with a craft knife or a pair of fine scissors. Wrap the calyx around the base of the flower, pressing the tape firmly to secure.

Buds

5 Roll a piece of white flower paste into a slender tube, leaving one end slightly more bulbous with a point. Make 5 cut marks lengthways down the tube with a craft knife to represent petals. Insert a moistened 30-gauge wire and roll the bud between your thumb and finger to taper the paste down the wire. Add a calyx.

Wedding Knife Spray

The flowers in the knife spray usually match those on the cake. Two or three flowers, some foliage and bows are sufficient.

Flowers

8 abutilon leaves (5 large, 3 small), page 28
2 jasmine buds, page 29
2 jasmine flowers, page 29
5 sprays dried gypsophila, page 9
2 carnations, page 28
1 double bounce bow, page 7

1 Start by taping together three small abutilon leaves. Tape down the first wire for approximately 1.5cm (¾ inch). Attach one leaf to the right of it and another 1cm (½ inch) under that on the left.

2 Attach a jasmine bud approximately 4cm (1½ inches) below the bottom leaf, and secure another bud immedi-

ately underneath that. Place a jasmine flower to the right of the bud and another just underneath to the left. Attach a piece of gypsophila on either side of the flowers and buds.

3 Position another piece of gypsophila under the jasmine flowers, one carnation in the centre and a large abutilon leaf to the right of the carnation.

4 Tape another piece of gypsophila to the left of the carnation, and place another carnation under that, slightly lower than the first. Secure a large abutilon leaf to the left of that.

5 Finally, tape a piece of gyp-

sophila under the two carnations, the ribbon loops under that, and three large leaves under these. Cut the wires, tape down the stem and attach the spray to the knife handle using florists' wire.

Rose

Long associated with love and romance, red roses make the perfect subject for a wedding spray.

Materials

24-gauge green wires
Flower paste
Egg white or gum glue
Paste and powder colours,
page 6

Equipment

Tweezers
Medium freesia cutter (F62,
A.P.) or template, page 47
Cocktail stick (toothpick)
Calyx cutter (248)
Dogbone tool
Rose leaf cutters and veiners

Flower

1 Make a hook in one end of a piece of 24-gauge wire. Make a cone of white flower paste (the size of which should be just smaller than the length of the petal), and attach this to the hooked wire with a little egg white or gum glue.

2 Roll out a piece of pale red flower paste quite thickly, and cut out four shapes using the freesia cutter or a template. Take one of the shapes (cover the pieces that are not being used), and use the blunt end of a cocktail stick to thin down the paste. To do this, start from the centre of each petal and use a rocking action out towards the left-hand side. Return to the centre and repeat for the right-hand side. When this has been completed, the petal should be between two and three times its original size and look like a rose petal. Work the remaining two petals in the same way, taking care not to damage the petal already worked.

3 Brush the white cone with a little egg white or gum glue. Take the shape in your hand and brush the middle petal and base with egg white or gum glue. Bring this petal forward and wrap it around the cone very tightly. (The middle petal is brought forward only for this first stage.) Paint the egg white or gum glue almost to the top of the remaining two petals. Stick the right-hand petal at the back of the cone and bring the left-hand petal forward to stick at the front. Wrap these two around, tucking one inside the other. Remove any surplus paste from around the base to neaten. (At this stage, if liked, a calyx can be attached and the flower used as a small bud.)

4 Take a second shape and work in the same way as before. Paint egg white or gum glue about one third of the way up the petals and wrap around the bud, again tucking one inside the other. Turn the edges of the petals outwards slightly; remove any surplus paste.

5 Repeat with the third shape, brush on some egg white or gum glue, and wrap the petals around the flowerhead; the shape should fit approximately three quarters of the way around the flower.

6 Cut one petal from the remaining shape, work as before, paint with egg white or gum glue, and place in the gap. Remove surplus paste.

Calyx

7 Roll out a piece of green flower paste thinly and cut out a calyx. Make one or two tiny cuts in the sides and soften the edges with a dogbone tool. Paint the centre of the calyx with egg white or gum glue, and place it at the base of the rose. Make a small oval shape from a piece of paste approximately the size of a pea; brush one end with egg white. Slide this up the wire and secure it behind the calyx.

Leaves

8 Use rose leaf cutters and veiners, and make according to the instructions on page 6. Tape into sprays of three or five leaves each, as required for the spray (right).

Rose Spray

Flowers

2 sprays rose leaves (5 leaves each)
2 rosebuds
6 three-quarter open roses
7 sprays rose leaves (3 leaves each)
5 gold acorns, page 36
3 open roses
1 double bounce bow, page 7

1 Take one of the five-leaf sprays and bend it into a curve towards you. Attach one of the smallest rosebuds.

2 Take two of the nearly open roses, secure one of them just beneath the bud at the bottom and the other to the right of this and slightly further back.

3 Place another nearly open flower behind the two already in place, in the centre, then arrange a set of three leaves and one acorn on each side of this rose. (Make sure you continue to curve the wires into a crescent shape.)

<table>
<tr><td>

4 Place one of the larger roses on the right, and secure another set of three leaves behind this.

5 Repeat steps 1–4, this time curving the wires in the opposite direction. Bend the

</td><td>

wires down and join the two sprays together to form a curve.

6 Secure the last rose at the top of the spray, in the gap. Add the remaining leaves and acorn. Attach the ribbon in the centre of the curve.

</td><td>

Opposite: Red Rose Cake (page 36)

</td></tr>
</table>

Red Rose Cake

Other coloured roses would look equally good on this simple cake. Try deep yellow roses for a golden wedding celebration.

Materials

20cm (8 inch) oval cake
Apricot glaze
750g (1½lb) marzipan (almond paste)
875g (1¾lb) cream sugarpaste (rolled fondant)
Clear alcohol (gin or vodka)
Cream royal icing

Equipment

20x25cm (8x10 inch) oval cake board
Icing smoothers
Piping bag
No. 42 piping tube (tip)
275cm (108 inches) 3mm wide ribbon to trim cake
92cm (36 inches) 15mm wide ribbon to trim cake board
Double-sided tape
Posy pick

Flowers

Rose Spray, page 35

Preparation

1 Brush the cake with apricot glaze, cover with marzipan, and allow to dry. Coat the cake board with sugarpaste, and set aside.

2 Brush the marzipan with clear alcohol and coat the cake with sugarpaste. When firm, place the cake on the cake board.

Decoration

3 Using cream royal icing and a no. 42 piping tube, pipe a snail's trail around the base of the cake. Attach three lines of narrow ribbon above this, securing with royal icing.

4 Make three matching bows and attach them to the side of the cake over the ribbon using a dot of royal icing for each.

5 Attach the broader ribbon to the edge of the cake board using double-sided tape.

6 Push a posy pick into the top of the cake. Carefully insert the spray of flowers into the pick, securing with a little royal icing if necessary.

Acorns

Gold-painted acorns make an attractive contrast to the deep red of the roses. Form a small piece of cream flower paste into an egg shape, and insert a moistened, hooked 26-gauge wire into the base and a small stamen into the top. Leave to dry. Push another slightly smaller piece of paste into an acorn cup mould. Hollow out and thin with a dogbone tool, and attach to the base of the nut with egg white or gum glue. Mould the cup gently to fit. When dry, paint with non-toxic gold paint.

Cymbidium Orchid

Orchids are unusual flowers that look most effective in wedding sprays.

page 6

Materials

24-gauge green wires
Flower paste
Paste and powder colours,
page 6
Egg white or gum glue
30-gauge white wires
Yellow textured powder
Claret/cyclamen liquid colour

Equipment

Orchid sets (19–21 and
344–345)
Orchid petal veiners
Dogbone tool
No. 000 sable paintbrush
Florists' tape

Column

1 Cut a piece of 24-gauge green wire approximately 10cm (4 inches) in length, and form a hook at one end.

2 Take a piece of cream flower paste approximately the size of a pea, and form this into a slender teardrop shape. Dip the wire in egg white or gum glue and attach the paste to this. Leave to dry overnight.

Throat and petals

3 Roll out some cream flower paste and cut out one shape with the orchid throat cutter. Frill the scalloped edge with a cocktail stick. Brush a small amount of egg white or gum glue on the two curved sides that are not frilled, and attach the throat to the column. Try to place the throat in the correct position at the first attempt – if it is repositioned too many times, this will leave a film of egg white on the surface of the column. Leave to dry.

4 Make three large and two narrow petals using the same method as for leaves (see page 6). Insert 30-gauge white wires, vein using orchid petal veiners and soften the edges with a dogbone tool. Dry with an inward curve.

5 Take a tiny piece of white paste, roll this into an oval shape and cut a line down the centre with a craft knife. Attach to the top of the column.

6 Roll a tiny piece of yellow paste into a thin sausage. Cut this in half lengthways,

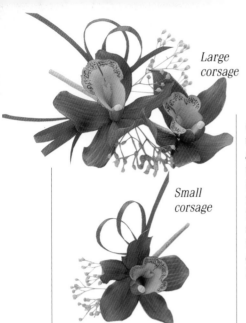

Large corsage

Small corsage

stopping just short of the end so it remains in one piece, but split. Attach this to the inside of the orchid throat with egg white or gum glue. Paint the top of it with egg white or gum glue and sprinkle a little yellow textured powder on to it. Tap out the excess powder.

7 With a no. 000 sable brush and claret/cyclamen liquid colour, paint in the dot pattern on the orchid throat. Dust the outside of the throat and the petals.

Assembly

8 Tape the three large petals to the throat, one at the top and the remaining two each side. Attach them behind at the base of the throat (to form a triangle). Tape the two narrow petals in the gaps. Tape down the stem and trim excess wire.

Small Orchid

Follow steps 1–3 on page 37, using the smaller cutter set (134–135). Make the petals using the five-petal cutter, vein, and soften the edges. Place a tiny amount of strong gum glue (page 46) behind the throat of the flower. Push the throat wire into the centre of the petals and slide the piece up behind the throat. Bring the petals forward; dry. Paint and dust as for the larger orchids.

Filler Flowers

Form a small piece of cream flower paste into a mexican hat shape, and cut out petals with a small calyx cutter (406). Hollow out the centre, and widen each petal in turn with a cocktail stick. Insert a moistened, hooked 28-gauge wire, pulling it through the centre. Push a stamen into the centre with tweezers. Dry, then dust.

Orchid Sprays

Three sprays are used to decorate the cake opposite.

Flowers

3 filler flowers
3 small orchids
1 figure-of-eight bow, page 7
4 sprays dried gypsophila, page 9
3 large orchids, page 37
4 double bounce bows with short tails, page 7

Top arch spray

1 First tape together the filler flowers, one above

the other, then attach a small orchid, slightly to one side. Place a second small orchid behind this and a third behind that at a slight angle. Bend the spray and attach it to the top of the perspex arch using florists' wire. Attach a figure-of-eight bow and a spray of gypsophila near the top of the spray.

Corsages

2 For the small corsages, take one large orchid and attach a piece of gypsophila and a bow to either the left or right. Note that the gypsophila and ribbon should be on the same side each time.

3 For the large corsage, tape two large orchids, one above the other, and attach a piece of gypsophila on either side of the gap between them. Tape in a bow on either side at the bottom of the spray.

Orchid Wedding Cake

The unusual colours of the orchids make this a perfect autumn wedding cake.

Materials

15cm (6 inch), 20cm (8 inch)
trefoil-shaped cakes
Apricot glaze
1.25kg (2½ lb) marzipan
(almond paste)
1.5kg (3lb) cream sugarpaste
(rolled fondant)
Clear alcohol (gin or vodka)
Cream royal icing

Equipment

20cm (8 inch), 28cm (11 inch)
round cake boards
Icing smoothers
Paper piping bags
Nos. 1.5 and 42 piping tubes
(tips)
92cm (36 inches) 3mm wide ribbon to trim cakes
Scriber
Garrett frill cutter
Cocktail stick (toothpick)
Perspex arch with posy pick
Florists' wire
Tweezers
117cm (46 inches) 15mm wide
ribbon to trim boards
Double-sided tape
C stand

Flowers

Top Arch Orchid Spray, page 38
6 Small Orchid Corsages,
page 38
Large Orchid Corsage, page 38

Preparation

1 Brush the cakes with apricot glaze, cover with marzipan, and allow to dry. Coat the cake boards with sugarpaste, and set aside.

2 Brush the marzipan with clear alcohol, and coat the cakes with sugarpaste. When firm, transfer the cakes to the cake boards.

Decoration

3 Using cream royal icing and a no. 42 piping tube, pipe a snail's trail around the base of each cake. Attach a line of narrow ribbon above this, securing with royal icing.

4 Scribe a line from the centre of the top edge of an outer curve of the cake to the bottom of a neighbouring indent, and another one from this indent, back up to the centre of the top edge of the next curve. Repeat on all sides of each cake. Roll out cream sugarpaste, cut Garrett frills and frill the edges with the blunt edge of a cocktail stick. Attach the frills to the cakes along the scribed lines, using a little alcohol.

5 Using cream royal icing and a no. 1.5 piping tube, pipe a random dot pattern on the bottom part of the sides of the cakes, under the frills.

Assembly

6 Make a hole in the centre of the small cake. Stand the arch over the hole and press the posy pick down into the cake. (The arch already has a hole in the base and a posy pick provided.) With a pair of tweezers, bring the flower heads in the top spray forwards.

7 With some royal icing, attach the small corsages in the indents of the two cakes. Place the large corsage in the posy pick. Attach the ribbons to the cake boards using double-sided tape. Carefully place the cakes on the stand.

Top arch spray

40

Longiflorum Lily

Longiflorum lilies are becoming very popular and look attractive arranged in a posy with plenty of foliage.

Materials

Flower paste
Paste and powder colours, page 6
26-gauge green wires
Egg white or gum glue
Stamens, optional
30-gauge white wire

Equipment

Florists' tape
Longiflorum cutters (569–570)
Dogbone tool
Lily veiners
Dresden tool

Pistil and stamens

1 Make the pistil as for the Casablanca Lily on page 8. Commercial stamens can be used or they can be made as for the Alstroemeria (see page 12), but make the ends elongated rather than drop-shaped and use 30-gauge white wires. Six stamens are required. Dust with lemon. Tape the stamens just underneath the tip of the pistil.

Petals

2 Roll out a piece of white flower paste, leaving a ridge of thicker paste down the centre. Cut out a wide petal and insert a moistened 30-gauge white wire as far as it will go. Soften the edges gently with a dogbone tool. Vein the petal with a veiner or dresden tool. Using the wider end of a dresden tool, curl the top of the petal inwards from the outside edge, then pull the tip back to curl outwards. Leave to dry slightly. Make two more petals in the same way, making sure they are firm enough to hold their shape but not completely dry. Tape them together around the pistil and stamens.

3 Cut out three narrow petals. These are not wired, but should have a small ridge of thicker paste at the base. Vein and shape in the same way, but make the backward curve more prominent. Brush the outside edges of these petals with egg white or gum glue, to about three-quarters of the way up, and attach in between the gaps of the first layer, making sure they are in line at the base of the flower. Leave to dry completely.

4 Dust the bases of the petals and the central vein on the outside of each petal with green. Steam over a kettle (see page 6). When completely dry again, dust the whole flower with white lustre.

Posy of Lilies

The Victorian posy is a popular shape for bouquets. Considered lucky, fresh rosemary brings a light, fresh feel to this posy.

Flowers

7 longiflorum lilies, page 41
9 fresh rosemary sprigs
6 sprays ivy leaves, page 18
6 double bounce bows with long tails, page 7

1 Hold one of the lilies in one hand and tape another three at even intervals around the central flower, bending the stems accordingly. Secure a piece of rosemary between each lily.

2 Slightly bend the wires of the three remaining lilies. Position these, one at a time, underneath the rosemary, forming the posy into a shape that represents half a ball.

3 Attach one sprig of rosemary in each remaining gap around the lilies.

4 Arrange six sprays of ivy, at even intervals, around the base of the posy. Finally, tape six double bounce bows at even intervals between the ivy.

Rose Bridal Favour

Traditionally, favours consist of small bags of sugared almonds – normally five, representing health, wealth, happiness, fertility and longevity.

Materials

Cream cotton thread
Fine florists' wire
28-gauge green wires
Egg white or gum glue
Flower paste
Paste and powder colours,
page 6
Yellow textured powder
5 sugared almonds
Small plastic saucer
Tulle
30cm (12 inches) ribbon

Equipment

Florists' tape (green)
Tweezers
Small freesia cutter (F63, A.P.)
or template, page 47
Cocktail stick (toothpick)
Dresden tool
Calyx cutter (248)
Wire cutters

Stamens

1 Make a cotton centre as for the Clematis on page 24. Open up the centre of the cottons and paint a little egg white or gum glue in the centre. Press in a tiny round piece of light green flower paste. Leave to dry. Brush the ends of the cottons with egg white or gum glue, and dip them in yellow textured powder.

Petals

2 Roll out a piece of pale yellow flower paste to medium thickness, and cut out five or six shapes with the small freesia cutter or a template. Working on one shape at a time (cover the pieces that are not being used), use the blunt end of a cocktail stick to thin down the paste. To do this, start from the centre of a petal and use a rocking action out towards one side. Repeat for the other side. Work the remaining two petals in the same way, taking care not to damage those already worked. When thinned, the petals should overlap one another. With a dresden tool, curl the petals inwards from the outside edge to the base.

Assembling flower

3 Brush some egg white or gum glue on the base of the paste and approximately one-third of the way up each petal. Wrap these around the stamens, ensuring the bottom of the petals comes below the base of the stamens. Remove any surplus paste from the base of the flower.

4 Take another shape and work in the same way as before. Join these to the first layer, trying to ensure that one petal does not sit immediately behind another. Continue with the remainder of the shapes, but curl the petals on the reverse side so that they curl downwards. Remember to remove the

surplus paste from the base with
each addition.

⟨5⟩ In order to achieve the
correct balance, a single
petal may need to be added dur-
ing progression of the layers. To
do this, cut out one shape and
cut off one of the petals. Work in
the same way as the other
petals and attach. Dry, then
dust.

⟨6⟩ Make the calyx as for the
Rose on page 32. For rose
leaves, see page 33.

Assembling posy

⟨7⟩ Arrange the almonds on
the plastic saucer. Stand
the saucer on a circle of tulle,
and gather up the tulle over the
almonds. Tie with ribbon.

⟨8⟩ Wrap a piece of florists'
tape around the stem of
the rose, starting directly underneath the calyx. Tape down the
stem for approximately 5mm (¼
inch), and then tape in a set of
three leaves. Continue down the
stem for another 2cm (¾ inch),
cut off the wires and tape.
Attach the rose to the favour by
tying it with the ribbon that is
already around the tulle. Make a
bow if desired.

Basic Recipes

Ready-made flower paste and edible glue are both available, but the following recipes work well.

Flower Paste

500g (1lb/3 cups) icing (confectioners') sugar
3 teaspoons gum tragacanth
5 teaspoons warm water
2 teaspoons liquid glucose
1 tablespoon white vegetable fat (shortening)
2½ teaspoons powdered gelatine
1 large egg white

1 Put the icing sugar in a heatproof bowl. Mix in the gum tragacanth. Warm the mixture in the oven on a very low setting.

2 Put the water in a heatproof bowl. Stir in the liquid glucose and vegetable fat, then sprinkle over the gelatine. Place this over a pan of hot water and heat through, stirring occasionally, until the ingredients have dissolved.

3 Warm the beater attachment of an electric food mixer. Transfer the sugar to the mixer bowl, and add the dissolved ingredients and the egg white. With the mixer on its lowest speed, beat until the mixture starts to come away from the sides of the bowl in strings.

4 Knead together into a smooth ball, then transfer to a polythene bag and store in an airtight container in the refrigerator. Leave for 24 hours before use.

Variation

This simpler method for making flower paste is based on bought pastello sugarpaste (*not* Regal-ice or rolled fondant). This flower paste does not need to be stored in the refrigerator, though it can be, if preferred. Unlike some other flower pastes, this is not prone to mould. Simply knead 1 rounded teaspoon of gum tragacanth into 250g (8oz) pastello sugarpaste. Place in a polythene bag in an airtight container and leave for 12 hours before use.

Gum Glue

This solution can be used instead of egg white.

1 teaspoon gum arabic
3 teaspoons boiling water

Place the gum arabic in a small, sterilized, heatproof jar. Add the boiling water, stir and leave to dissolve.

Variations

For a stronger 'glue', break off a small amount of flower paste and mix it to a paste with the gum arabic solution. This will make a strong, tacky adhesive.

For a 'glue' that will remain clear and is not prone to discolouring, combine ¼ teaspoon carboxymethylcellulose (CMC) with 5 tablespoons warm water in the same way as for the gum arabic solution.

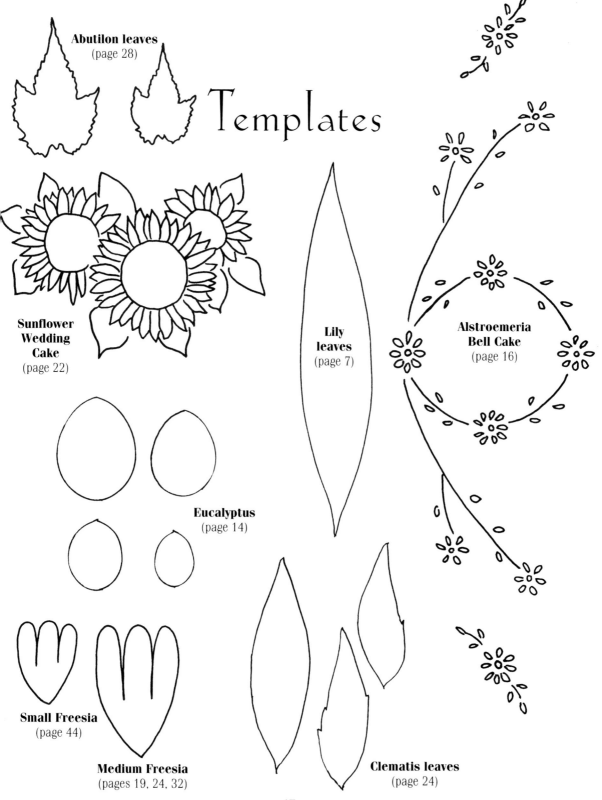

Abutilon leaves
(page 28)

Templates

Sunflower Wedding Cake
(page 22)

Lily leaves
(page 7)

Alstroemeria Bell Cake
(page 16)

Eucalyptus
(page 14)

Small Freesia
(page 44)

Medium Freesia
(pages 19, 24, 32)

Clematis leaves
(page 24)

For further information on products used
within this publication, please contact our
Customer Services team.

Culpitt Limited
Jubilee Industrial Estate
Ashington
Northumberland
NE63 8UQ

Tel 0845 601 0574
customer.services@culpitt.com